SPACE
REVEALED

Written by
ALEX BARNETT

LONDON, NEW YORK,
MUNICH, MELBOURNE, and DELHI

PROJECT EDITOR SIMON HOLLAND
SENIOR DESIGNERS JIM GREEN, ADRIENNE HUTCHINSON
AND OWEN PEYTON JONES
PHOTOSHOP ILLUSTRATOR MARK LONGWORTH
MANAGING EDITOR LINDA ESPOSITO
MANAGING ART EDITOR SOPHIA M.
TAMPAKOPOULOS TURNER
CATEGORY PUBLISHER SUE GRABHAM
ART DIRECTOR SIMON WEBB
PICTURE RESEARCHER HARRIET MILLS
JACKET DESIGNER BOB WARNER
DTP DESIGNER TOBY BEEDELL
PRODUCTION CONTROLLER DULCIE ROWE
CONSULTANTS DR. JACQUELINE MITTON
AND PETER BOND

First American Edition, 2004
04 05 06 07 08 10 9 8 7 6 5 4 3 2

Published in the United States by DK Publishing, Inc.
375 Hudson Street, New York, NY 10014
Copyright © 2004 Dorling Kindersley Limited

Library of Congress Cataloging-in-Publication Data
Barnett, Alex
  Space / written by Alex Barnett.-- 1st American ed.
      p. cm. -- (DK revealed)
Summary: Contains a survey of space, illustrated with photography of
planets, astronomical discoveries, and both human and robotic space
explorations. Transparent acetate spreads reveal details not normally
visible to the naked eye.
Includes index.
  ISBN 0-7566-0305-6
  1. Toy and movable books--Specimens. 2. Outer space--Juvenile
literature. 3. Astronomy--Juvenile literature. [1. Outer space.
2. Astronomy. 3. Toy and movable.] I. Title. II. Series.
  QB500.22.B37 2004
  520--dc22
                                                          2003021667

Color reproduction by Colourscan, Singapore
Printed in China by Leo Paper Group

Discover more at
www.dk.com

CONTENTS

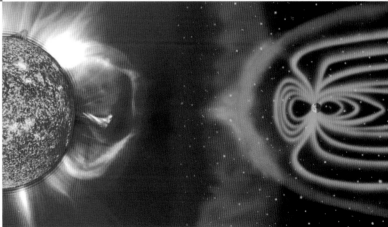

EARLY ASTRONOMERS

In *c*. 750 BC, Babylonian astronomers made calculations to do with the rising and setting of the Moon. They used this information to create the very first almanacs—tables that recorded the movements of the Sun, Moon, and planets. Almanacs of this kind could be used to make calendars, and to predict events such as the eclipses of the Sun and Moon.

BEYOND EARTH

A Babylonian calendar carved on a stone tablet

HUMANS HAVE ALWAYS LOOKED UP at the sky. Sometimes, they did so for practical reasons, such as finding out what time of day it was or whether it was a good period for planting crops. At other times, it was to seek guidance or tell fortunes. Many ancient civilizations had beliefs associated with the heavens. The Ancient Egyptians thought bright stars represented gods and goddesses, and buried the pharaohs in a method designed to help them join these gods in the heavens. As people got better at measuring and looking at the sky, they began to discover how the cosmos works and where our place is within it. Theories once put us at the center of the universe, before we realized that our planet, Earth, is only a very tiny part of it. Our quest for knowledge continues, but we can now travel beyond Earth and use new technology to look back at our own world, as well as out into space.

The construction of Stonehenge began about 5,000 years ago. The largest stones had to be transported from many miles away

The upright stones are called sarsens, and those across the top are called lintels

STONEHENGE

Early farmers tracked the changing seasons by following the position of the Sun in the sky, as the year moved between summertime and wintertime. Stonehenge, in England, was possibly used as a giant calendar, with stones set up to align with important positions of the Sun during the year. It is also possible that it was used to tell the time, or for religious ceremonies. We will never know for sure.

PTOLEMY

This picture of the Greek astronomer Ptolemy shows him contemplating the universe. He lived in Alexandria, Egypt, in the 2nd century AD and wrote down the ideas of the Ancient Greeks, who believed that the Earth was a perfect sphere at the very center of the universe. Ptolemy also named 48 patterns of bright stars in the sky—known as constellations—including Orion.

The top part of a V-2 rocket carried a small payload (cargo) instead of a bomb

COPERNICUS

People thought the Earth was at the center of the universe until Nicolaus Copernicus (AD 1473–1543) put forward the idea that the Sun was at the center, and that the Earth moved around it. He had no proof, but this new theory encouraged observers and mathematicians to try to explain how the planets might travel around the Sun. Within 150 years, it had been proved that the Sun is at the center of our planetary system.

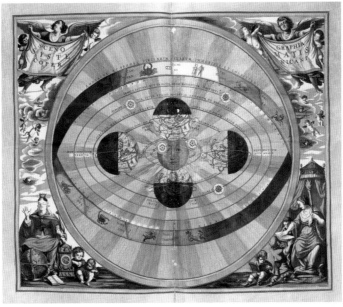

A replica of Galileo's telescope

Galileo's famous sketches of the Moon showed the craters on its surface

GALILEO

The telescope was invented at the start of the 1600s, and scientists began to use it to observe the sky. Galileo, the best known of those 17th-century observers, recorded what he saw using low-power telescopes. His observations of Venus showed that it moves around the Sun. He also drew sketches of the Moon, although Englishman Thomas Harriott was probably the first person to make a map of its surface.

This gantry supported the rocket until launch

Scientists observing the launch of an adapted V-2 rocket in 1950

ROCKET DEVELOPMENT

In the centuries that have passed since Galileo, our understanding of technology has leapt forward, producing better telescopes and instruments to help us study the universe. Those same advances also led to the development of the rocket. Originally used to carry bombs, rockets were later adapted for peaceful use—as a means for us to leave the confines of Earth and travel into space.

Strelka

Belka

SOVIET SPACE DOGS
On November 3, 1957, the Russian dog Laika ("barker"), on board *Sputnik 2*, became the first animal to be sent into space, where she survived for seven days. In 1960, Belka ("squirrel") and Strelka ("little arrow") spent a day in space inside *Sputnik 5* and successfully returned to Earth.

FIRST MAN IN SPACE
On April 12, 1961, a Russian test pilot called Yuri Gagarin became the first human to orbit the Earth. He traveled in a ball-shaped capsule, *Vostok 1*, orbiting at a speed of 17,000 mph (27,400 km/h). Gagarin died in a plane crash in 1968, before he got a chance to return to space.

SPACE RACE

AFTER WORLD WAR II (1939–45) the US and the Soviet Union used technology from the German V-2 rocket to build missiles. They realized that a rocket able to carry a bomb halfway around the world might also be used to lift people and machines into space. The Space Race began when the Soviets launched their *Sputnik* satellite in 1957. President Kennedy's statement that America intended to go to the Moon increased the competition between these two rival sides as they strove to demonstrate the superiority of their technology. The achievements of these two superpowers were remarkable, considering that the computers of the time were less powerful than today's basic calculators.

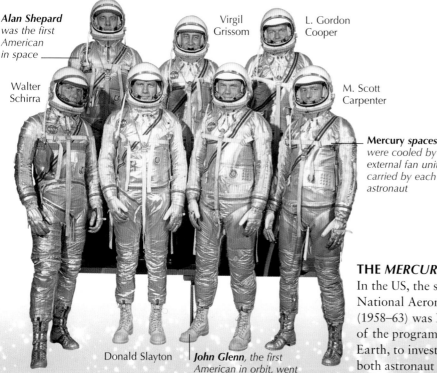

Alan Shepard was the first American in space

Virgil Grissom

L. Gordon Cooper

Walter Schirra

M. Scott Carpenter

Mercury spacesuits were cooled by an external fan unit, carried by each astronaut

Donald Slayton

John Glenn, the first American in orbit, went around the Earth three times

FIRST WOMAN IN SPACE
On June 16, 1963, 26-year-old Valentina Tereshkova became the first woman in space, spending almost three days inside her *Vostok 6* spacecraft. She completed 48 orbits of the Earth— at the time, this was more than the total number of orbits completed by all the US astronauts put together.

THE *MERCURY* PROGRAM
In the US, the space program was coordinated by NASA, the National Aeronautics and Space Administration. *Mercury* (1958–63) was NASA's first manned space program. The goals of the program were to orbit a manned spacecraft around Earth, to investigate our ability to live in space, and to recover both astronaut and spacecraft safely. NASA chose seven astronauts to take part, and six *Mercury* flights were made.

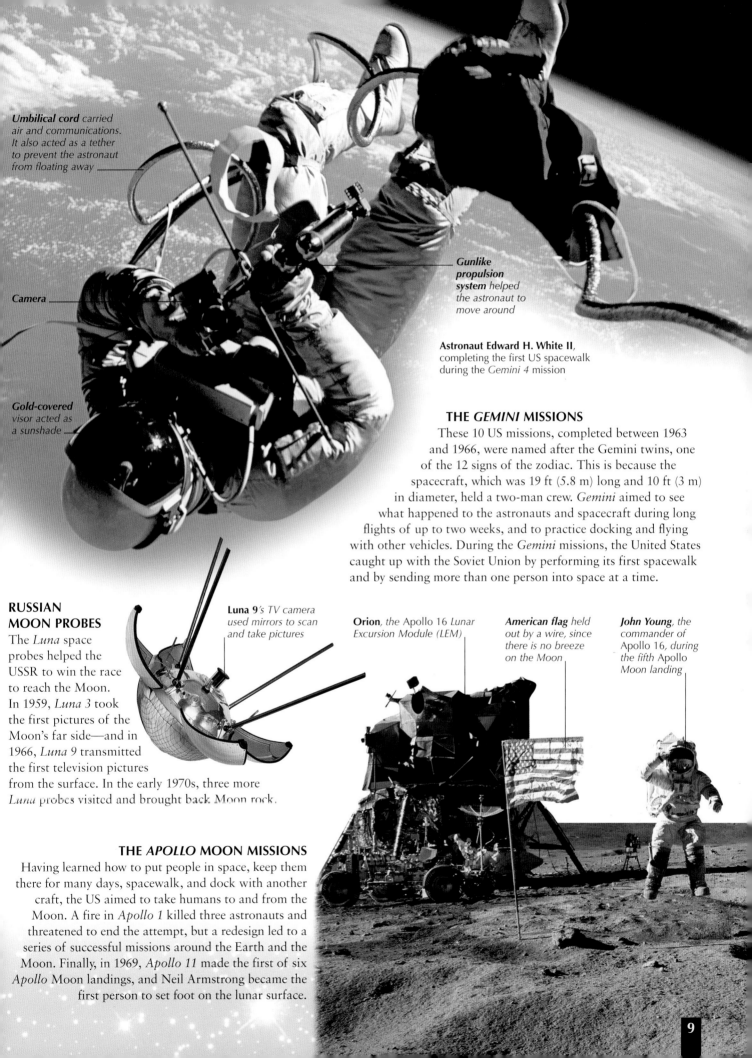

Umbilical cord carried air and communications. It also acted as a tether to prevent the astronaut from floating away

Camera

Gold-covered visor acted as a sunshade

Gunlike propulsion system helped the astronaut to move around

Astronaut Edward H. White II, completing the first US spacewalk during the Gemini 4 mission

THE GEMINI MISSIONS

These 10 US missions, completed between 1963 and 1966, were named after the Gemini twins, one of the 12 signs of the zodiac. This is because the spacecraft, which was 19 ft (5.8 m) long and 10 ft (3 m) in diameter, held a two-man crew. Gemini aimed to see what happened to the astronauts and spacecraft during long flights of up to two weeks, and to practice docking and flying with other vehicles. During the Gemini missions, the United States caught up with the Soviet Union by performing its first spacewalk and by sending more than one person into space at a time.

RUSSIAN MOON PROBES

The Luna space probes helped the USSR to win the race to reach the Moon. In 1959, Luna 3 took the first pictures of the Moon's far side—and in 1966, Luna 9 transmitted the first television pictures from the surface. In the early 1970s, three more Luna probes visited and brought back Moon rock.

Luna 9's TV camera used mirrors to scan and take pictures

Orion, the Apollo 16 Lunar Excursion Module (LEM)

American flag held out by a wire, since there is no breeze on the Moon

John Young, the commander of Apollo 16, during the fifth Apollo Moon landing

THE APOLLO MOON MISSIONS

Having learned how to put people in space, keep them there for many days, spacewalk, and dock with another craft, the US aimed to take humans to and from the Moon. A fire in Apollo 1 killed three astronauts and threatened to end the attempt, but a redesign led to a series of successful missions around the Earth and the Moon. Finally, in 1969, Apollo 11 made the first of six Apollo Moon landings, and Neil Armstrong became the first person to set foot on the lunar surface.

MOONWALK

FOOTPRINTS STILL MARK our adventures on the Moon, where there is no wind to disturb the lunar sand. From 1969 until 1972, the *Apollo* missions put 12 astronauts on the surface of the Moon to perform various experiments and learn about living in space. *Apollo 17* carried the last of the astronauts, who collected 243 lb (110 kg) of rock, took more than 2,000 photographs, and spent 22 hours walking on another world. The two moonwalkers each had their own, custom-made spacesuit, which had 22 layers to protect them from the jagged rocks, micrometeoroids, extremely hot and cold temperatures, and the radiation from the Sun.

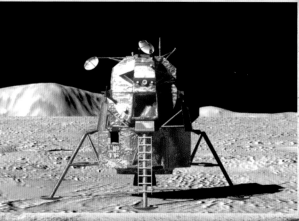

LUNAR EXCURSION MODULE (LEM)
The *Apollo 17* LEM, named *Challenger*, was the part of the spacecraft that landed on the Moon. It became the astronauts' base during their stay. A TV camera on the surface captured the top part blasting off into space, carrying Eugene Cernan and Harrison Schmitt to rejoin Ronald Evans inside the command module.

EXPLORING AN *APOLLO* SUIT

1 **Helmet:** *a gold visor with top and side eyeshades protected eyes from blinding sunlight. Red stripe indicates commander*

2 **Instrument panel:** *for monitoring the life-support systems, communications, and power. A camera was also worn here*

3 **Lunar drill:** *used to make 15-ft- (4.5-m-) deep holes in the ground to put detectors in, and for digging up rock samples*

4 **Collection bag:** *the mission commander had one to carry tools, equipment, and samples of Moon rock*

5 **Communications headset:** *astronauts kept in touch with each other, and with mission control, using radio communications*

6 **Portable life-support system:** *carried the batteries, oxygen for breathing, water for cooling, and got rid of carbon dioxide*

7 **Pressure garment assembly:** *a tight rubber suit, beneath the protective layers, with joints to allow the astronaut to move*

8 **Liquid cooling garment:** *special underwear with water pumped through cooling tubes to maintain a comfortable temperature*

MOON BUGGY

The *Apollo 15, 16,* and *17* LEMs each carried a car. This battery-powered lunar rover was stored as a "flat pack" for the astronauts to unpack and assemble on the Moon. It had a top speed of 9 mph (14 km/h) and helped the *Apollo 17* moonwalkers to travel 22 miles (35 km) and collect many types of Moon rock.

SPACEWALK SIMULATION

Handling objects while wearing a large spacesuit can be very difficult. Astronauts cannot move as easily in space as they can on Earth. One way to simulate spacewalking is to train inside a large water tank. The buoyancy that the astronauts experience in the water is a little like weightlessness. The tank at the Johnson Space Center in Houston is large enough to contain the entire International Space Station. Astronauts learn how to use tools and equipment specially designed for space, which always have plenty of handholds, hooks, and grips.

SPACE PEOPLE

ASTRONAUTS COME FROM ALL kinds of backgrounds. Some are scientists, while others are pilots, engineers, or doctors. But they have all gone through a fiercely competitive process to be selected as an astronaut, so that one day they might get an opportunity to go into space. There are more than one hundred active astronauts, but about half have not yet flown. Before going into space, astronauts have to understand the jobs of the thousands of other people upon whom their lives will depend. Trainee astronauts work in mission control and research mission experiments. They learn about life support and about their spacecraft, and spend many hours keeping up-to-date with their training. The really hard work begins when they are finally selected for a mission.

VR TRAINING

Repairing a telescope or putting together pieces of the International Space Station takes a lot of practice. Astronauts only get one chance to do the job for real, so many train using virtual reality (a computer-simulated environment). During a VR simulation, several astronauts can interact with each other.

The astronauts are floating against the padded roof of the KC135 aircraft

ZERO GRAVITY TRAINING

It is possible to experience weightlessness for a brief time on Earth, and so test out experiments and astronauts. This is done by flying in the "vomit comet." NASA uses a KC135 plane that flies in a path like a giant roller coaster. Each time the plane dives downward, the astronauts on board experience valuable seconds of zero gravity. One in three gets "spacesick."

Hot water goes in this valve to rehydrate the food

Nuts and dried fruit

Honeycomb

Drinks to mix with hot or cold water

SHUTTLE SIMULATOR

Like a giant version of an aircraft simulator, the Space Shuttle Simulator teaches astronaut pilots how to fly the Shuttle orbiter. Inside this replica flight deck, astronauts practice landing on different runways. They also practice docking and undocking with the International Space Station, maneuvers to launch satellites, and various orbiter escape drills.

EATING

Most food taken into space is dehydrated (dried out), so that it uses up less room and lasts longer. Astronauts use hot and cold water, stored in special dispensers, to prepare the food before they eat it. The onboard menu is very varied and includes dishes from many different parts of the world. Spicy food is popular, since astronauts lose their senses of smell and taste after some time in space.

EXERCISING

Straps hold the astronaut onto the exercise machine so that he does not float off

In space, the astronauts are not working against the force of gravity, so their muscles and bones start to waste away. To make sure that they can still stand up when they get back to Earth, astronauts have to exercise for at least one hour every day. There is a range of exercise machines on board the International Space Station.

Sleeping bags help to keep astronauts' arms from floating around while they are asleep

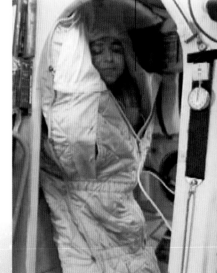

SLEEPING

As they orbit Earth, astronauts see many sunrises and sunsets per day. This is why they have to have a timetable that tells them when to sleep. Most astronauts say they sleep well in a weightless environment, although they cannot escape the fan noise. Fans are needed to move the breathed-out carbon dioxide away from the mouths of the astronauts, so that they do not suffocate.

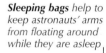

SPACE NATIONS

Many nations send satellites into space, and there are now more than 30 orbital launch sites around the world. These include locations in India, Japan, and Europe, as well as in Russia and the US. But the number of nations that can launch people into space is much smaller. China joined that number in 2003, when it sent astronaut Yang Liwei into orbit inside *Shenzou 5*.

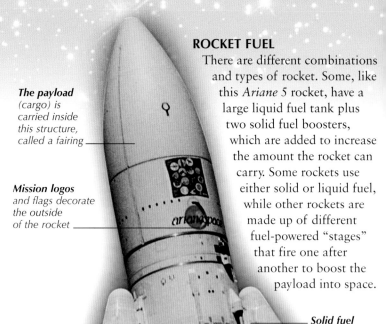

The payload (cargo) is carried inside this structure, called a fairing

Mission logos and flags decorate the outside of the rocket

ROCKET FUEL

There are different combinations and types of rocket. Some, like this *Ariane 5* rocket, have a large liquid fuel tank plus two solid fuel boosters, which are added to increase the amount the rocket can carry. Some rockets use either solid or liquid fuel, while other rockets are made up of different fuel-powered "stages" that fire one after another to boost the payload into space.

Solid fuel boosters are used to give the rocket extra power

ROCKET POWER

Tens of thousands of people from all over the world can claim to be rocket scientists. Such people are those who design, build, and launch the rockets and spacecraft that carry people and satellites into space. During one year, the Space Shuttle and the Russian *Soyuz* craft may go up a few times, but these manned flights are vastly outnumbered by orbital rocket launches. In less than 50 years, rocket power has progressed from being able to launch a football-sized satellite to delivering payloads the size of a school bus and weighing many tons. The satellites that these rockets put into orbit affect our everyday lives, helping us to watch the weather, learn about the universe, and find our way on Earth when we are lost.

The Sea Launch rocket

ROCKET COMPANIES

If anybody wants to launch a satellite, they will always have a choice of companies that will offer them a rocket to do so. They might launch it on a *Soyuz*, a *Proton*, an *Ariane*, a *Delta*, or an *Atlas*—to name but a few. One company, called Sea Launch, even launches satellites from a converted oil rig in the Pacific Ocean.

The powerful **Vulcain engine** *also helps steer the rocket*

An Ariane 5 rocket produces enough thrust to transport a nine-ton payload

SATELLITES

Satellites are built to be tough. Almost shaken apart during the launch, they then end up in the cold vacuum of space. They range from tiny "microsats," used for simple jobs, to big space telescopes and Earth-observing platforms. Many different types of satellite are launched, such as those used for communications, weather-watching, and military purposes.

The external tank holds the fuel that powers the Shuttle's main engines

The solid rocket boosters land in the ocean, to be recovered after use

ERS-1, *the European Remote Sensing Satellite, was launched in 1991. It looked at each part of the Earth once every 35 days, but it is now out of operation*

MISSION CONTROL

The job of getting people or satellites into space, and controlling their operations, happens at mission control. Procedures are more complex for human spaceflight, and there are usually at least two control centers. If one fails, another is able to take over the operations.

The mobile launch platform carries the Shuttle stack to the launch pad

The tail aileron helps to steer the Shuttle as it glides in to land

SHUTTLE LAUNCH

This Space Shuttle orbiter has spent three months being prepared for launch. Every inch has been checked, and the rockets are now attached. From the massive vehicle assembly building, the Shuttle moves at 1.2 mph (2 km/h) to the launch pad where the tanks will be fueled and final checks made before liftoff.

SHUTTLE LANDING

It takes about one hour for the Shuttle to travel from Earth's orbit to its landing site—a special runway, which is twice as long and wide as the average airport runway. The Shuttle is basically a huge glider and cannot make a second attempt at landing. Therefore, the pilot has to get it right the first time.

Drag parachutes help to slow the Shuttle down once it has made the landing

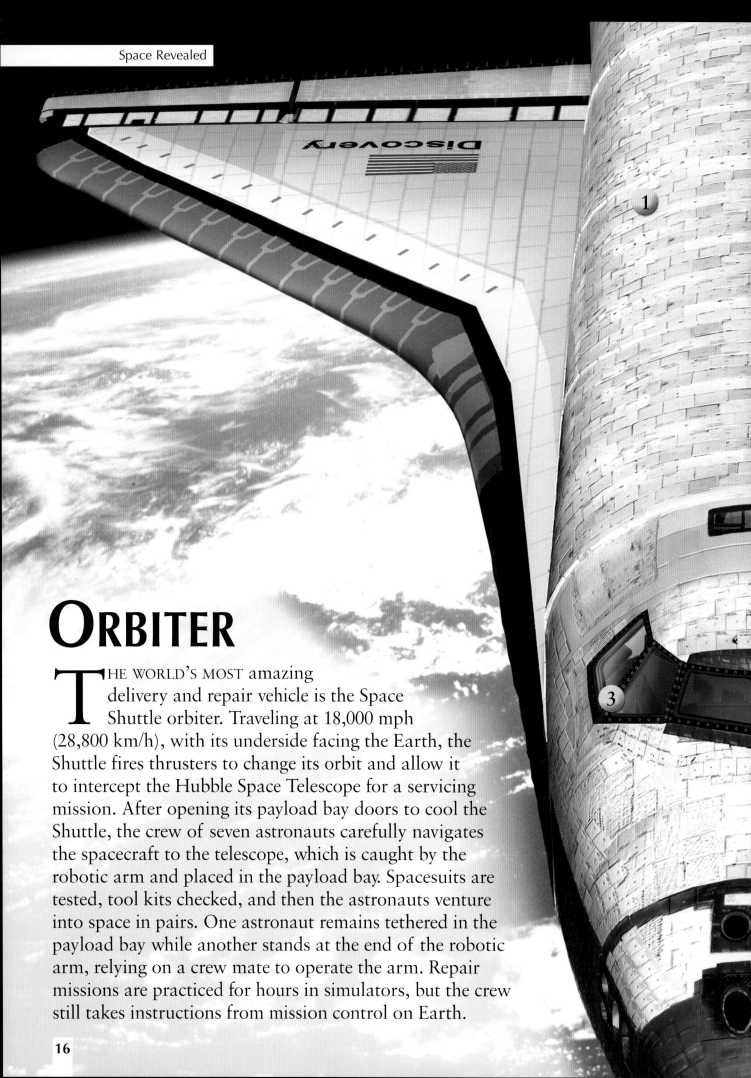

Discovery

1

3

ORBITER

THE WORLD'S MOST amazing delivery and repair vehicle is the Space Shuttle orbiter. Traveling at 18,000 mph (28,800 km/h), with its underside facing the Earth, the Shuttle fires thrusters to change its orbit and allow it to intercept the Hubble Space Telescope for a servicing mission. After opening its payload bay doors to cool the Shuttle, the crew of seven astronauts carefully navigates the spacecraft to the telescope, which is caught by the robotic arm and placed in the payload bay. Spacesuits are tested, tool kits checked, and then the astronauts venture into space in pairs. One astronaut remains tethered in the payload bay while another stands at the end of the robotic arm, relying on a crew mate to operate the arm. Repair missions are practiced for hours in simulators, but the crew still takes instructions from mission control on Earth.

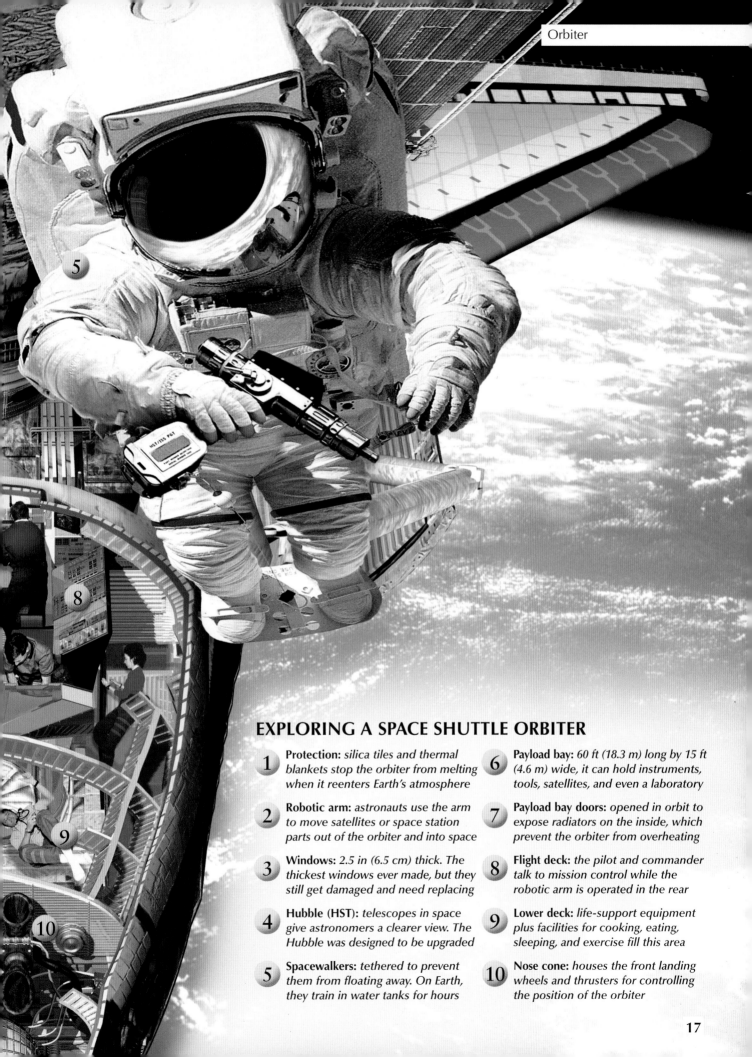

5

8

9

10

EXPLORING A SPACE SHUTTLE ORBITER

1 **Protection:** *silica tiles and thermal blankets stop the orbiter from melting when it reenters Earth's atmosphere*

2 **Robotic arm:** *astronauts use the arm to move satellites or space station parts out of the orbiter and into space*

3 **Windows:** *2.5 in (6.5 cm) thick. The thickest windows ever made, but they still get damaged and need replacing*

4 **Hubble (HST):** *telescopes in space give astronomers a clearer view. The Hubble was designed to be upgraded*

5 **Spacewalkers:** *tethered to prevent them from floating away. On Earth, they train in water tanks for hours*

6 **Payload bay:** *60 ft (18.3 m) long by 15 ft (4.6 m) wide, it can hold instruments, tools, satellites, and even a laboratory*

7 **Payload bay doors:** *opened in orbit to expose radiators on the inside, which prevent the orbiter from overheating*

8 **Flight deck:** *the pilot and commander talk to mission control while the robotic arm is operated in the rear*

9 **Lower deck:** *life-support equipment plus facilities for cooking, eating, sleeping, and exercise fill this area*

10 **Nose cone:** *houses the front landing wheels and thrusters for controlling the position of the orbiter*

SHUTTLE LABORATORIES

The US Space Shuttle's cargo bay is designed to hold pallets and containers storing instruments and equipment, but it can also be used as a temporary research station. Some of the equipment flown on the Shuttle includes telescopes and experiments designed to study both the Earth and space. Occasionally, the whole bay is taken up with a laboratory such as *Spacelab*, *Neurolab*, or the four-person *Spacehab*.

Velcro hooks help the astronauts to stay at their laboratory workstations

SPACE STATIONS

Small spacecraft, such as the *Apollo* capsule, could only support astronauts for a couple of weeks. In order to find out how humans could live and work in space, more permanent homes were needed. The Soviets were the first to put a station in space with *Salyut 1*, in 1971. In 1973, the US *Skylab* followed. It was five times larger than *Salyut* and helped to establish the types of research that could be done in space. As relations improved between the US and the former Soviet Union, the prospect of a truly international space station started to look more likely. The Russian *Mir* space station provided a glimpse of the future, with missions involving astronauts from many countries, and a chance to try out new technologies.

SPACELAB CREW

The European Space Agency's reusable laboratory, *Spacelab*, was flown many times inside Shuttle cargo bays between 1983 and 1997. It allowed astronauts to do experiments in the near-weightless environment of microgravity. There is no "up" or "down" in space, so the equipment racks are located in the floors, walls, and ceilings.

THE *MIR* SPACE STATION

Launched in 1986, *Mir* became a testing ground for international cooperation in space. Traveling inside the Shuttle or the Russian *Soyuz* craft, 104 people of many nationalities visited *Mir* during its lifetime. A separate craft delivered supplies. After 75 spacewalks, 16,500 experiments, and 600 new technologies, *Mir* was abandoned in 2000.

American docking module

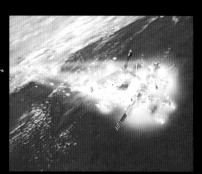

MIR BURN-UP

Mir was expected to last five years, but completed nearly 15. Its end came in March 2001, when a docked, unmanned craft fired its engines to move the space station out of Earth's orbit. After burning up over Fiji, the last pieces dropped safely into the Pacific Ocean.

SPACE PLANTS

The environment of microgravity, experienced in space, is a great place to do experiments that cannot be performed on Earth. We need to see how plants grow without gravity so that we can learn how to grow food in space. Other experiments include growing crystals to use in new drugs for treating cancer and diabetes, and the development of new metals for computers.

'Yecora Rojo' 83 days old

The wheat uses the light to decide which way is up in space

THE INTERNATIONAL SPACE STATION (ISS)

The International Space Station is a collaboration between 16 countries. When complete, the ISS will have six laboratories and will take up about as much space as a five-bedroom house. At least another 20 launches are needed to put the remaining pieces into space. In October 2000, the station was properly manned—and since then, for the first time in history, human beings have maintained a permanent presence in space.

About 44,000 sq ft (4,000 sq m) of solar panels provide electrical power for the ISS

ISS CONSTRUCTION

Rockets and the Shuttle deliver trusses, solar panels, and modules into orbit, and it is the astronauts who form the ISS construction crew. Working in very difficult conditions, inside bulky spacesuits and armed with special tools, the astronauts move pieces into place using both the Shuttle's robotic arm and the ISS's own "Canadarm." So far, more than 50 spacewalks from the Shuttle and the ISS, totaling about 320 hours of work, have gone into the building process.

The Shuttle's robot arm provides a movable working platform, so that astronauts can reach different parts of the ISS

Astronauts rely on portable life-support systems when spacewalking

The ISS's "Canadarm" was supplied by the Canadian Space Agency

The tops of mountains provide the greatest places on Earth for looking at the sky. The best sites are those where the telescopes, housed inside large observatories, will usually sit above the clouds. At this altitude, the sky is clear and the air is steady. These conditions allow astronomers to observe very fine details that they could not see if they were nearer to sea level. Astronomers have to bid for the time they can spend using the world's largest telescopes, such as this one in Las Campanas, in Chile.

VIEWING SPACE

WE CANNOT PUT A STAR or galaxy in a laboratory to examine it, so astronomers have always had to make good use of their intelligence—and the technology available to them—to find out about things in space. All objects give off electromagnetic radiation. By studying that radiation, astronomers can gather a lot of information about an object, such as how hot it is, what it is made of, and how far away it is. They can even tell how fast it is traveling through space. There was a time, in the 1800s, when people thought we would never know what the universe is made of, or how big it is. Today, astronomers have all kinds of tools at their disposal, from balloons and satellites to giant telescopes, and each new tool brings us an even greater amount of information about the universe in which we live.

X-RAY IMAGES

Even if astronomers can see an object in visible light and radio waves, they might also take a picture of it using X-rays—because an X-ray image can show up its hotter, higher-energy features. This image is of the same object as the one made using radio waves (below).

Gamma rays
0.01 nm and smaller

X-rays
0.01 nm to 10 nm

Ultraviolet
10 nm to 400 nm

Visible light
400 nm to 700 nm

Most types of electromagnetic radiation are measured in nanometers (nm). 1 nm is equal to one billionth of a meter

Infrared
700 nm to 1 mm

Microwaves
1 mm to 30 cm

Radio waves
30 cm and greater

THE ELECTROMAGNETIC SPECTRUM

Electromagnetic radiation is a form of energy that spreads through empty space at the speed of light. It travels in the form of individual "wave-packets," called photons. The smaller the waves in the packet, the more energy the photon carries. The electromagnetic spectrum is the full range of wavelengths that photons can carry—ranging from low-energy radio, with long waves, to high-energy gamma rays, with the shortest wavelengths.

RADIO IMAGES

The cooler parts of stars, gases, and galaxies all send out radio waves. Astronomers can detect and "map" large structures, such as the remains of this exploded star, using their radio telescopes. Radio waves from the Sun warn us when it is about to get active.

SPACE-BASED OBSERVATORIES

The atmosphere that surrounds and covers the Earth protects us from dangerous radiation such as ultraviolet rays and X-rays. This also means that if astronomers want to collect that kind of radiation from space, they need to get above the atmosphere with a space-based observatory. Often, many nations work together to launch a large space telescope, such as the Chandra X-Ray Observatory, shown here.

A telescope cover protected the mirrors during launch

The X-rays are collected by bouncing them off a set of nested mirrors

Thrusters allow the astronomers to steer and aim the telescope

Thermal blankets protect the telescope from the extremely hot and cold temperatures of space

Different instruments collect the X-rays and use them to create images

Solar panels provide power for the onboard computers and detectors

ROCKETS AND BALLOONS

Sending large telescopes into space is expensive. This is why astronomers perform a lot of their research by sending detectors (sensing apparatus) into the upper atmosphere, to the edge of space, using either a balloon or sounding rocket. A sounding rocket is a rocket designed to gather data at high altitudes and radio it back to Earth. Many new detectors are tested in this way before they are used on big telescope missions. This balloon is carrying a gamma-ray camera to take images of an exploding star.

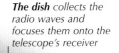

The dish collects the radio waves and focuses them onto the telescope's receiver

RADIO TELESCOPES

Radio waves can be as large as a football field, so to collect them you need a really big dish. But it is not practical to build dishes as large as this. Instead, astronomers use a special technique that involves building several telescopes, such as the 27 dishes of the Very Large Array in New Mexico. These dishes are spread out over 22 miles (36 km) and combine their radio signals to create one image.

Galaxies contain large "clouds" of gas and dust—the material from which new stars are formed. Some of the gas came from stars that lived a long time ago, and then exploded or blew off their outer layers. Clusters of stars are created when a passing shockwave—perhaps from a nearby exploding star—causes dense clumps, called cores, to form inside the cloud.

LIFE OF A STAR

IN A CLEAR NIGHT SKY, IT MIGHT be possible to see about 2,000 stars. They look tiny, but only because they are very far away from us. If we could see them up close, they would look like our Sun—a massive ball of incredibly hot gas. The force of gravity plays a big part in the birth, life, and death of a star, and each star's lifespan and manner of death depend on how massive it is (how much material it contains). Most stars are about the same size and mass as the Sun, or smaller and less massive, but there are also some bigger, more massive stars. At least half the stars in the universe belong to binary systems, in which two stars are kept close together by gravity and orbit around each other.

The Eagle Nebula, a star-forming region

A PROPLYD
In a star-forming cloud, a small clump of gas begins to attract more gas. This increases the clump's mass, which also increases its gravitational pull. The increasing gravity attracts more gas, and so it goes on. As the gas piles in and squashes together, it gets very hot and starts to glow. This "baby star" is known as a proplyd.

A YOUNG STAR
Gravity continues to pull the gas inward. Eventually, the force of all that gas pressing downward squashes the middle of the baby star, so that it gets hot enough for nuclear fusion reactions to begin. The energy flowing outward from these nuclear reactions at its core prevents the star from collapsing any further.

A MAIN SEQUENCE STAR
The energy flowing outward, from the core, eventually balances out the inward pull of gravity. Once this has occurred, the star settles down and steadily "burns"—through nuclear reactions—its hydrogen into helium. Aside from flares and starspots, nothing dramatic happens. The most massive stars use up their fuel in just millions of years, while the least massive burn for billions of years.

SOLAR SYSTEMS

In 1984, a dusty disk was observed around a nearby star called *Beta Pictoris*. The discovery was made by a satellite designed to take pictures of things that give off infrared radiation. The dust was being heated up by the star, and glowed brightly. This was the first time that astronomers had seen proof that newborn stars might have disks of material moving around them, which could develop into new planets.

The dust spreads out in an elongated band, seen edge-on in this image

The bright, central star is covered up to highlight the faint dust

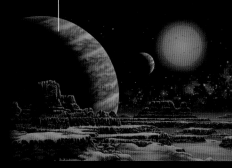

Massive, Jupiter-like worlds are the only extrasolar planets that astronomers have detected so far

EXTRASOLAR PLANETS

In 1995, astronomers found evidence of "exoplanets," planets that move around other stars. We have not yet seen these planets, but we know they exist because their gravity causes their central star to "wobble" a little. Astronomers can measure this wobbling to determine how massive the planets are.

The outer layers are drifting off into space. This is known as a planetary nebula

The inner layers glow, mainly due to the ultraviolet radiation coming from the dying star

A "white dwarf" is the name for the collapsed core of the original star

STAR DEATH

All stars eventually run out of the hydrogen fuel in their core. In the case of middle-sized, Sunlike stars, once the energy stops flowing outward the pull of gravity takes over again. This gravitational pull "squeezes" the star until it is hot enough in the middle to convert helium into carbon. A huge rush of energy is then released, which makes the star unstable and causes it to swell up into a "red giant" star. Gradually, it throws off layer after layer of its material into space.

SUPERNOVA

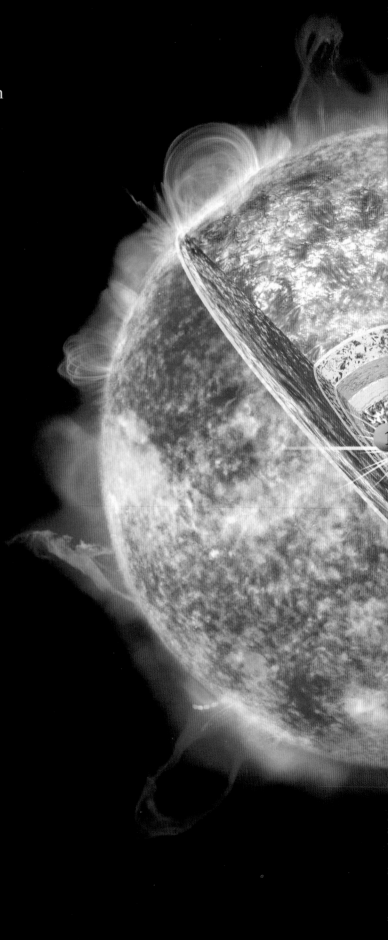

MASSIVE STARS GO OUT with a bang. Much more massive than the Sun, they only live for millions, rather than billions, of years. They rapidly consume all the material they can draw on as fuel for the nuclear reactions that generate energy and keep them shining. In the dense, incredibly hot core of a massive star (much smaller than it is shown here), nuclear "burning" transforms the original hydrogen into different elements, which build up in layers from the center. Finally, the middle of the core turns to iron. But iron cannot "burn" to make energy. With no energy flowing from its center, the core implodes, triggering a tremendous supernova explosion.

SUPERNOVA IN THE LARGE MAGELLANIC CLOUD
Exploding stars shine so brightly that they often outshine an entire galaxy. In 1987, a star exploded in the Large Magellanic Cloud, which is a small galaxy 170,000 light-years from ours. This was the closest supernova to occur since the invention of the telescope. These images show the Large Magellanic Cloud before and after the star's dramatic death.

EXPLORING A RED SUPERGIANT

(1) Iron core: *silicon inside the star burns to create a tiny iron core. Once this occurs, the star has only a few days left before it explodes*

(2) "Onion" layers: *very big stars generate many different nuclear reactions, each happening inside a different layer of gases*

(3) Cooler, outer layers: *the energy flowing outward, from the center, keeps all this gas from being pulled inward by gravity*

(4) Surface layers: *far out from the center of the star, the gases are much cooler—about 45,000°F (25,000°C) in temperature*

(5) Collapsing core: *in one second, the core collapses from being 6,000 miles (10,000 km) wide to just 6 miles (10 km) wide*

(6) "Ejecta": *during the final seconds of the star's life, lots of elements are created. This star dust might one day form planets and beings*

(7) Shockwave: *traveling at roughly 6,000 miles (10,000 km) per second, the shockwave slams into the surrounding gas and makes it glow*

(8) Energy: *a supernova explosion can give out as much energy as the Sun produces over the course of nine billion years*

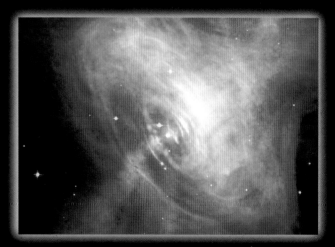

PULSAR IN THE CONSTELLATION OF TAURUS
In AD 1054, Chinese astronomers observed a brilliant supernova—in the area circled (above)—among the stars of Taurus. It could even be seen during the day. Today, we can still detect the spinning remains of the dead star at the center of a gas cloud. This is known as a pulsar. As the pulsar spins, it sends out beams of radiation, including radio waves, light, and X-rays.

THE SUN AND THE PLANETS

This diagram is a basic map of our solar system. It is not to scale. Each planet is labeled to show its average distance from the Sun. The distances between objects in space are huge, and are measured here in millions of miles (Mm) and millions of kilometers (Mkm).

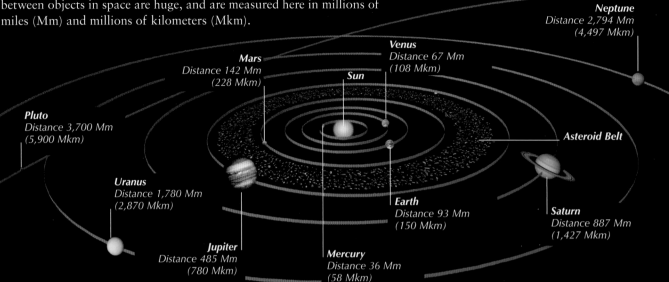

Neptune
*Distance 2,794 Mm
(4,497 Mkm)*

Venus
*Distance 67 Mm
(108 Mkm)*

Mars
*Distance 142 Mm
(228 Mkm)*

Sun

Pluto
*Distance 3,700 Mm
(5,900 Mkm)*

Asteroid Belt

Uranus
*Distance 1,780 Mm
(2,870 Mkm)*

Earth
*Distance 93 Mm
(150 Mkm)*

Saturn
*Distance 887 Mm
(1,427 Mkm)*

Jupiter
*Distance 485 Mm
(780 Mkm)*

Mercury
*Distance 36 Mm
(58 Mkm)*

SUN AND SOLAR SYSTEM

IT IS OFTEN HARD TO THINK OF THE SUN as a star, but that is what it is. It is a very average, middle-sized star. The Sun was born almost five billion years ago, and a dusty disk of material around it formed the nine planets that make up the solar system. We rely on the Sun's energy for life on Earth, so finding out about it and how it keeps shining is very important. Spacecraft take pictures of it and gather information, and what we learn from our nearest star helps us to understand the more distant ones. Every second, our Sun converts tons and tons of matter into pure energy through nuclear reactions. It will eventually use up this fuel and burn itself out, but not for another five billion years or so.

*Prominence, a huge
arc of gas in the
Sun's atmosphere*

ACTIVE SUN

Powered by the release of a burst of magnetic energy, huge flares erupt above the Sun's surface and send streams of high-energy particles and radiation into space. The Sun goes through cycles, reaching a peak of activity once every 11 years. Astronomers can see its eruptions and active spots better by using ultraviolet light to take pictures such as this one.

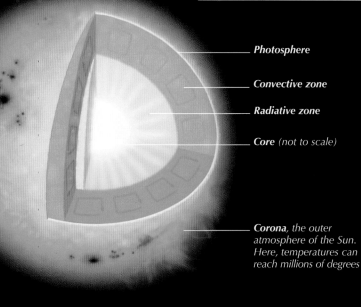

Sunspots are magnetic storms on the surface of the Sun. Sometimes, they are several times the size of the Earth

Photosphere

Convective zone

Radiative zone

Core (not to scale)

Corona, the outer atmosphere of the Sun. Here, temperatures can reach millions of degrees

INSIDE THE SUN

The Sun is a massive ball of seething-hot gas. Nuclear reactions are going on at its core, where hydrogen atoms are crashing together to become helium. These reactions give out energy, and that is what keeps the star shining. The nuclear energy takes 300,000 years to make its way from the core to the surface of the Sun.

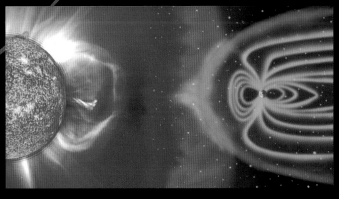

THE EARTH'S MAGNETIC FIELD

The Earth has a magnetic field that acts like a shield, pushing away the charged particles that are flung at us by the Sun's violent outbursts. This field protects our planet from the worst of the deadly radiation. Fortunately, the Sun is about 93 million miles (150 million km) away from us.

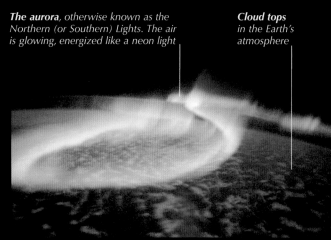

The aurora, otherwise known as the Northern (or Southern) Lights. The air is glowing, energized like a neon light

Cloud tops in the Earth's atmosphere

THE AURORA (NORTHERN OR SOUTHERN LIGHTS)

When clouds of particles from the Sun blast against Earth's magnetic shield, they trigger geomagnetic storms, which can disrupt electricity supplies and endanger astronauts and satellites. The disturbed magnetic field flings the particles trapped in it toward the Earth, making the upper air glow in an oval region around the poles. This is called the aurora.

SOHO is the size of a small car and needs these huge solar panels to power it

The spacecraft's name, SOHO, stands for the Solar and Heliospheric Observatory

UNDERSTANDING THE SUN

A small fleet of satellites and spacecraft have become our solar weather forecasters. They monitor the Sun for storms and help us to understand the daily workings of our nearest star. This satellite, *SOHO*, sits in a place between the Earth and the Sun where it can give us an early warning of events occurring in the Sun's atmosphere (the corona).

ASTEROIDS

Like the leftover rubble at a construction site, the asteroids of the solar system are pieces of rock that did not become part of a planet. Most of them circle the Sun in a huge band called the Asteroid Belt, which lies between Mars and Jupiter. Some asteroids follow paths that take them very close to the Earth. This one is called Eros.

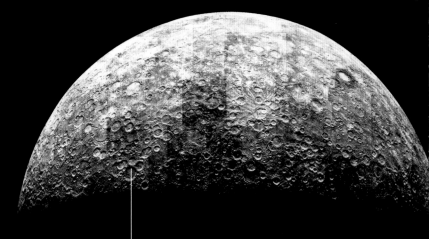

Spacecraft have only shown us half of Mercury's surface

MERCURY

Mercury, the closest planet to the Sun, is covered with craters—scars caused by collisions with other pieces of rock. At first glance, it looks a little like the Moon. With no wind or rain to disturb them, the craters will remain for millions of years. Mercury roasts by day at a temperature of 788ºF (450ºC), which plummets to an unbelievably chilly -328ºF (-200ºC) at night.

INNER PLANETS

THE PLANETS OF THE SOLAR SYSTEM were created from the disk of dust and gas that surrounded the newly born Sun. Close to the young star it was very hot, and only the rocks and metals in this material were able to stand the heat. Four small, "inner" planets formed, in which the molten metal sank to the center and the lighter rock floated nearer the outside. The early solar system was a violent place, where showers of debris bombarded the newly formed planets, chiseling out craters and shattering the land. Incoming icy comets dropped water onto the rocky planets, and gases escaped from the rocks to form atmospheres. But this is where the similarities between Mercury, Venus, Earth, and Mars end. Spacecraft and probes send back data from our near neighbors, and we are only just beginning to learn their full stories.

VENUS

Venus is slightly smaller than the Earth, and people often call it Earth's twin. Earth and Venus both have an atmosphere that contains clouds. Venus's swirling atmosphere is extremely cloudy and presses down with about 90 times more force than the Earth's atmosphere. The atmosphere on Venus is unbreathable, as it is made up of poisonous carbon dioxide gas.

BELOW THE CLOUDS

Venus is the hottest planet in the solar system, thanks to the thick atmosphere that smothers it. Mercury is closer to the Sun, but has no atmosphere to hold on to its heat. The carbon dioxide in Venus's atmosphere traps the heat from the Sun like a greenhouse. A spacecraft called *Magellan* used radar to map out the surface of Venus, where there are rocks and volcanoes that glow at more than 842ºF (450ºC).

The clouds of Venus contain droplets of sulfuric acid

EARTH, THE BLUE PLANET

Not too close to the Sun, and not too far away, Planet Earth's location is just right for liquid water to exist on its surface. With its plate movements, earthquakes, and volcanoes, Earth is a very active world—but it was much more chaotic in its early days, when it was home to massive volcanoes and was frequently bombarded by rocks from space.

EARTH AND ITS MOON

In its early history, the Earth probably turned much faster and may have had no moon. It was then hit by a very large rock, causing pieces of debris to spin off into space. This material collected in Earth's orbit and later formed the Moon. The Moon's gravitational pull on the Earth then slowed down its rotation.

The dark areas on the Moon are called seas, but they do not contain water

The Earth's atmosphere is about 300 miles (500 km) deep from the surface to its thinnest, outer layers

Mars has massive volcanoes. The largest, Olympus Mons, is higher than Mount Everest

MARS, THE RED PLANET

Mars is just over half the size of Earth, and its year is twice as long, but one Martian day is only about half an hour longer than ours. Mars is a dry, dusty planet with a very thin, unbreathable atmosphere made up of carbon dioxide. The temperature rarely rises above freezing during the summer. Water in the form of ice exists in the polar caps and frozen in the rocks. Primitive life-forms might be able to survive on Mars, or may have been able to in the past.

Two stereoscopic cameras are the "eyes" of the Mars Rover. They will be used to take detailed pictures

A powerful antenna will enable signals to be sent directly back to Earth or relayed via a spacecraft orbiting Mars

The Mariner Valley is the largest canyon we know of. It is large enough to stretch across the US

ROBOTIC EXPLORERS

Before we send humans on long and dangerous journeys to the planets, it makes sense to find out all that we can about them using robots. Some robots, such as this *Mars Exploration Rover*, which landed in 2004, are about the size of a small car. Others, such as the *Beagle 2* mission to Mars, are not much bigger than a car tire.

JUPITER

Jupiter is two-and-a-half times more massive than all the other planets put together. If it were only 80 times more massive, it would be a small star. Circled by more than 60 moons, Jupiter is famous for its colored cloud tops and the Great Red Spot—a 300-year-old hurricane with a width that is about twice the diameter of Earth.

Europa

THE GALILEAN MOONS

Four of Jupiter's moons, discovered by Galileo in 1610, are worlds in their own right. Europa may have oceans of water beneath its icy crust, as may Callisto. Io is the most volcanic place in the solar system, and cratered Ganymede is larger than the planet Mercury.

The Great Red Spot

OUTER PLANETS

GASSY AND ICY MATERIALS WERE BLOWN back by the heat of the newborn Sun. These gases and ices then gradually collected around rocky cores to form the planets known as the gas giants—massive worlds traveling on orbital paths billions of miles from the Sun. All four gas giants have rings, although only Saturn's are easily visible. Jupiter and Saturn, the fifth and sixth planets from the Sun, were known to ancient observers, but Uranus and Neptune, the seventh and eighth, were only discovered when later astronomers scanned the skies using their telescopes. Spacecraft and robotic probes have visited these planets during the last 30 years, sending back information, but no craft has yet gone to examine the outermost rocky planet, Pluto. It remains, for now, a secret to us.

Saturn's ring system, discovered in 1655 by Christiaan Huygens

False-color images show up the different cloud bands. Saturn is actually a creamy color

SATURN

This is the second-largest planet and probably the most famous, thanks to its spectacular system of rings. When he first observed Saturn in 1610, Galileo mistook the rings for two moons. Saturn spins rapidly, which makes it bulge in the middle. It measures 12,400 miles (20,000 km) more from side to side than it does from top to bottom.

COMETS

Most of the icy, rocky leftovers from the formation of the solar system live in the Oort Cloud, a cloud of objects orbiting at great distances from the Sun. When disturbed, these "dirty snowballs" may shift to different paths that bring them into the inner solar system. As they get closer to the Sun the ices turn to vapor, and we see the streams of gas and dust as two tails that form behind each comet.

URANUS

In 1781, the astronomer William Herschel discovered Uranus, the first of three planets that were not known to the ancients. Uranus is a strange world. It is tilted on its side, so that each of its poles spends a period of time facing the Sun as the planet orbits it. Each hemisphere (side) of Uranus gets up to 42 years of night, followed by 42 years of daylight.

Uranus's thin rings contain material that is as black as coal dust

Storms rage in Uranus's swirling atmosphere, just as they do on all the gas planets

NEPTUNE

Neptune's vivid, blue-green color is due to the methane gas in its atmosphere. The white flecks visible in this picture are the planet's fast-moving clouds, which are driven by 1,240-mph (2,000-km/h) winds. One of Neptune's moons, Triton, is a very unusual place. It is home to geysers and pink "snow," and is probably the coldest place in the solar system.

The Great Dark Spot, a large storm, was seen in 1989—but by 1994 it had vanished

A Voyager craft's television camera could read a newspaper headline 0.6 miles (1 km) away and take very long-exposure pictures

Signals now take more than 12 hours to get from Earth to the Voyager crafts' dishes

The transmitter signals have 20 billion times less power than a digital watch battery when they reach Earth

The 43-ft (13-m) boom on each craft carries sensitive instruments. It was unfurled after launch

THE VOYAGER MISSIONS

Launched in 1977, the two Voyager spacecraft took advantage of a rare alignment of the planets to explore the outer solar system. Voyager 1 visited Jupiter and Saturn, while Voyager 2 passed by all four gas planets, and their combined missions made tens of thousands of new discoveries. The craft are now heading into interstellar space and are currently more than 8 billion miles (13 billion km) away from Earth.

Some of the instruments on the Voyager spacecraft are still performing scientific tests—but the crafts' power will run out in around 2020

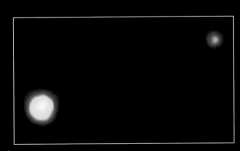

PLUTO AND CHARON

This is one of the best images of tiny Pluto and its large moon, Charon. Pluto was not discovered until 1930. It is called a planet, but astronomers now know that it is probably the largest of a big group of rocky, icy worlds—known as Kuiper Belt Objects—that orbit the Sun beyond Neptune. Pluto is smaller than at least seven other moons in the solar system, and has a stretched-out orbit that sometimes takes it inside the path of Neptune.

SATURN MISSION

Robots can venture where no person can. *Cassini-Huygens* is a spacecraft designed to survey Saturn and its largest moons. Three space agencies combined to build the craft. It was launched on October 15, 1997, and will reach Saturn in 2004. *Cassini* gathered speed on its 2 billion-mile (3.2 billion-km) journey by using the gravity of Venus, Earth, and Jupiter to "slingshot" it along. At Saturn, *Cassini* will release the *Huygens* probe, which is to land on Titan, the planet's biggest moon. If it survives the trip, the probe will work for up to half an hour before its batteries run down. *Cassini* will orbit Saturn for four years, sending back around 300,000 images and enough data to fill more than 400 CDs.

EXPLORING THE *CASSINI-HUYGENS* MISSION

1 **Cassini:** *largest-ever interplanetary craft. It is 23 ft (7 m) wide and has 12 different science instruments*

2 **Saturn:** *a gas planet. It is less dense than water, and so would float if placed in an enormous bathtub*

3 **Moons:** *Saturn has 31 moons. The gravity of some, called shepherd moons, keeps ring particles in line*

4 **Titan:** *it may have seas of liquid ethane and methane, and an atmosphere of nitrogen gas*

5 **Atmosphere:** *made mostly of hydrogen and helium, with wind speeds of 1,100 mph (1,800 km/h)*

6 **Molecular hydrogen:** *most of Saturn is made of hydrogen in different forms. In this layer, the hydrogen atoms are joined together in pairs*

7 **Metallic hydrogen:** *here, the hydrogen is being squashed into a metallic liquid state by the huge pressure exerted on it*

8 **Rocky core:** *has a temperature of about 21,000°F (12,000°C). Saturn gives out more heat than it gets from the Sun*

9 **Rings:** *made up of billions of icy rocks of different sizes. The rings are about 0.6 miles (1 km) thick*

10 **Huygens:** *has instruments to collect samples and work out what makes up the Titan air*

THE BIG BANG THEORY

Nobody was around to see how the universe began, but scientists study the clues and try to work out how things happened. Most astronomers believe that the universe started as something very small, and that it "blew up" shortly after its creation—like a balloon being filled with air very quickly. This period of very rapid expansion is known as cosmic inflation.

UNIVERSE

STUDYING EVERYTHING THAT EXISTS sounds like an impossible task, but that is what astronomers are effectively doing when they look at the universe. The universe includes everything there is, from the tiniest atom to the largest galaxy, and from the stuff that gives out light to the mysterious "dark matter." Galaxies are made up of stars, gas, and dust, and they gather together in galaxy clusters. Those clusters lump together to form galaxy superclusters, and in between the superclusters are enormous voids of empty space. Astronomers sometimes describe this structure as being a bit like a gigantic sponge. The universe is expanding—and as space stretches, the galaxies move farther apart. The universe is so vast that astronomers measure distances using the speed of light as their ruler. Light travels at 186,000 miles per second (300,000 kilometers per second), and the light that telescopes capture from very distant objects has often been traveling through space for billions of years.

This dark matter "map" was created by combining 39 separate Hubble Space Telescope images

The brightest section contains most of the dark matter, and most of the visible matter

DARK MATTER AND DARK ENERGY

Only about 5 percent of all the matter (stuff) in the universe is visible. We know that the invisible matter is there because we can measure its effects on the stuff that we can see. What makes up this "dark matter" is a mystery, but astronomers do have some ideas. These experts also talk about "dark energy" when they are trying to explain how the universe behaves. Both ideas are at the forefront of today's research.

A massive black hole *lies at the center of the Milky Way galaxy*

A pair of colliding, spiral galaxies

GALAXIES
The main visible building blocks of the universe are galaxies, which come in many shapes and sizes. Elliptical galaxies, shaped like footballs, are made up of old stars and contain little interstellar gas and dust. Others can be beautiful spirals. Some galaxy shapes are thrown into chaos by huge amounts of star formation, or because they have merged with another galaxy.

The Sun *is located two-thirds out from the center, along a spiral arm called the Orion Arm*

THE MILKY WAY
Our star, the Sun, lives in a large "star city" along with billions of other stars. This place is called the Milky Way galaxy. The oldest stars form a hub at the center, while younger stars are born in clusters along the spiral arms that surround the middle. The spiral arms contain lots of gas and dust. Circling the galaxy are globular clusters, which are ball-shaped groups of up to 100,000 stars.

Arecibo radio telescope, *Puerto Rico, used for SETI experiments. The dish is 1,000 ft (300 m) across*

Detectors *are suspended by large cables above the collecting dish*

SUPERMASSIVE BLACK HOLES
Lurking at the center of probably every large galaxy is a supermassive black hole at least a million times the mass of the Sun. Astronomers are not sure how these black holes form, but they are surrounded by massive, swirling disks of gas. This gas gives off X-rays, which we can detect and take pictures of. This image shows many X-ray sources in the general area of our galaxy's center.

SEARCH FOR EXTRATERRESTRIAL INTELLIGENCE (SETI)
We could, perhaps, find intelligent life-forms in the universe by listening for their radio signals. Astronomers point their telescopes at stars like the Sun, which might have planets suitable for life moving around them. We do not know exactly how to "tune in" to these signals, so computers scan the radio bands and listen for things that lifeless matter could not produce.

LUNAR MINING

As Earth runs out of natural resources, companies might develop ways of extracting them from the vast amounts of material on the Moon and asteroids. Lunar mining bases would be mostly robotic, with machinery for cutting into the rock, automated processing plants, and a "space truck" to haul the products back to Earth. These materials might also be used to build spacecraft, or be transported for use on other planets.

NEW HORIZONS

HUMANKIND HAS ACHIEVED A GREAT DEAL since 1957, when the first satellite was launched. During this short period of time, technology has made amazing advances—so it is interesting to consider how far we might get in the next 50 years. Most people believe that we will have stepped on Mars by that time, and some think there will be bases on the Moon and people living in huge cities orbiting the Earth. Our robot explorers may have examined all the planets and moons, and our technology might have improved so that we can travel more quickly and cross great distances in space in months rather than years. These ideas may sound like science fiction, but that is also how earlier generations viewed the notion of going to the Moon.

Mars spacesuits and vehicles are tested by the Mars Society researchers

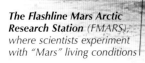

The Flashline Mars Arctic Research Station (FMARS), where scientists experiment with "Mars" living conditions

PUTTING PEOPLE ON MARS

Space agencies and private organizations are developing ways for humans to visit Mars. Mars is the most Earth-like of all the planets, but going there is not a simple project. The journey is dangerous and will take many months—and it will be a major challenge to survive on and explore the planet. Getting home again will be just as difficult.

ION PROPULSION

A spacecraft moves because the exhaust, blowing in one direction, propels the craft in the opposite direction. Inside an ion engine, charged particles are created and shoot out of it at 60,000 mph (100,000 km/h), causing the spacecraft to move. This "fuel" is cheaper and is used in small quantities, so ion engines are more efficient than traditional engines and can run for longer. At the moment, ion engines cannot move heavy payloads, but are ideal for small probes and satellites. *Deep Space 1* was the first space mission to use an electric, ion-propelled engine.

The star tracker keeps the spacecraft on course

Deep Space 1 uses charged xenon gas particles as its fuel

A special design enables the aircraft to fly at very high altitudes

The White Knight *aircraft was created by Scaled Composites LLC, one of the contenders for the X Prize. This craft is designed to launch the rocket (below)*

THE X PRIZE

Technology has been greatly advanced as a result of competitions, in which a prize was given as a reward. The X Prize is a competition that is designed to encourage private space tourism, and more than 20 teams are currently taking part. The goal for each team is to build and launch a spaceship that can carry three people to 60 miles (100 km) above the Earth and then return safely. This feat must then be repeated, using the same spacecraft, within two weeks. The winners will collect $10 million.

SpaceShipOne is the rocket that will carry the three passengers

A large scaffold holds the huge solar sails. Each sail is bigger than a football field

SPACE TOURISTS

Currently, the only way you can hitch a ride to space is to pay for it. The cost is around $20 million! Mark Shuttleworth is an African businessman who could afford to become the second official "space tourist." But if the X Prize is successful, in 10 years' time people could be planning to spend their vacations in space.

SOLAR SAILS

Another way we could travel in space is by using sunlight. We do not feel the force or pressure from sunlight in our everyday lives because things on Earth, such as gravity and the wind, drown out these effects. In space, however, where things can move freely, the force of sunlight reflecting from large, lightweight solar sails could be harnessed to move a spacecraft.

INDEX

ACKNOWLEDGMENTS

**Dorling Kindersley would
like to thank:**
Dorothy Frame for the index,
Alyson Lacewing for proofreading,
Sarah Mills for DK Picture Library
research, and Margaret Parrish
for Americanization.

**The publisher would like to
thank the following for their
kind permission to reproduce
their photographs:**
Key: a = above; b = below;
c = center; l = left; r = right;
t = top; ace = acetate

Olivier Boisard – Conseil: 37bl.
**Bridgeman Art Library,
London/New York:** Giraudon 7tcr.
Lynette R. Cook: ©2000 23cra.
Corbis: M. Dillon 6b; Myron Jay
Dorf 35ca; NASA 27cr; NASA/Roger
Ressmeyer 3c, 5clb, 30tl, 30bl;
Alain Nogues/Sygma 15tr; Enzo

& Paolo Ragazzini 7cla; Roger
Ressmeyer 5cla, 20tl, 21cl, 21bc.
DK Images: British Museum 6tl.
European Space Agency: 15cra;
CNES/Arianespace-Service Optique
CSG 14r; NASA/Jean-Paul Kneib
(Observatoire Midi-Pyrénées,
France/Caltech, US) 34clb. **Galaxy
Picture Library:** Robin Scagell
25 ace. **Getty Images:** AFP 14tl;
Oleg Nikishin/Stringer 37br. **David
Malin Images:** Anglo-Australian
Observatory 24clb, 24 ace. **NASA:**
page borders t&b, 4r, 8bl, 9br,
10–11 (background), 10–11 ace
(background), 12tl, 12cl, 12br, 13tl,
13clb, 15cla, 16-17, 16-17 ace,
18tl, 18cr, 18bl, 19ca, 19cra, 19b,
21tr, 22br, 24-25c, 24-25c ace,
29tr, 31cra, 32-33, 32-33 ace,
36tl; CXC/SAO 20ca;
CXC/SAO/MIT/F. K. Baganoff et al.
35cbr; A. Fruchter/ERO Team/STScl
23bl; /Jeff Hester & Paul Scowen

Arizona State University 22cl; The
Hubble Heritage Team, STScl,
AURA 35tl; JPL/Caltech 28tl, 29br,
29cal, 30car, 31cb, 37tl; STScl/
C. R. O'Dell (Rice University)
22bl; STScl/Erich Karkoschka
(University of Arizona) 31tl; X-ray:
CXC/ASU/J. Hester et al, Optical:
HST/ASU/J. Hester et al: 25crb.
National Space Centre, Leicester:
33cr. **NOAO/AURA/NSF:** T. A.
Rector, B. A. Wolpa, M. Hanna,
KPNO 0.9-m Mosaic/Copyright
WIYN Consortium, Inc., all rights
reserved 2, 39. **NASA:**
NSSDC/GSFC/NASA: 28cb, 31bcl.
Royal Astronomical Society: 7clb.
Scaled Composites: 36-37c. **Science
Photo Library:** David P. Anderson,
SMU/NASA 28bc; S. Durrance &
M. Clampin 23tl; D. Golimowski,
Mark Garlick 22cb, 22bc, 27tc;
Steele Hill/NASA 5crb, 27cl; Jerry
Lodriguss 30cr; NASA 5tr, 7r, 9t,
15br, 28tr; Novosti 8tl, 8tr, 8cbr;
NRAO/AUI/NSF 20bc; David Parker
35bl; Erich Schrempp 34tr; US

Geological Survey 29clb; Detlev
Van Ravenswaay 18cb. **Courtesy
of Sea Launch:** 14bl. **Courtesy of
SOHO/EIT Consortium. SOHO
is a project of international
cooperation between ESA
and NASA:** 27bcr; 26-27b.
Videocosmos.com: 13br.
Dr. Robert Zubrin: 36b.

Jacket images:
Front: NASA (background)
Back: NASA/A Fruchter/ERO
Team/STScl tl; Hubble Heritage
Team, STScl/AURA tr.
Spine: NASA/Dryden Flight
Research Center.

All other images
© Dorling Kindersley
www.dkimages.com

Every effort has been made
to trace copyright holders of
photographs. The publishers
apologize for any omissions.